MINISTERING TO THE LORD

A Vision, A Search,

All Scripture quotations in this volume are taken from the *King James Version* of the Bible, unless otherwise stated.

Dedicated to:

E.S. Hoopes, Jr., and family, with my best love. Through their love and friendship my life has been enriched and my ministry strengthened and increased.

ISBN 0-89274-153-8
Printed in United States of America
Copyright © 1980 by Roxanne Brant
All Rights Reserved

Table of Contents

Other Titles by the Author

Rivers of Evidence
The Growing Power of Faith
How to Test Prophecy, Preaching and Guidance
8 Biblical Ways to Receive Healing
Recent Angelic Visitations
Transported by the Holy Spirit (co-authored)
The Jim Kaseman Story (co-authored)
Knowing God's Will for Your Life

*See page 95 for details
and information on ordering.*

Preface

The truths in this little book have revolutionized my life and ministry. They are from Him. After years of teaching and preaching this message, I feel more strongly than ever, that if we would only put Him and our ministry to Him first, we would see the Church of Jesus Christ arise with a new glory, ablaze with His fire and consumed with a holy passion to do His will.

Too long have we worshiped today's idols. We have exalted our traditions above His gospel and the institution above her Lord. We need to repent. We have let everything else arise in the Church, and now it is time to "Let God arise, let His enemies be scattered" (Psalm 68:1) as we turn wholeheartedly to Him to minister to Him and do His will.

This little book by no means covers the details on the subject of *Ministering To The Lord*. It is written merely to present what Jesus has made so real to me. It is also written because He has told me to write it. I hope that it will change your life as it has changed mine.

God bless you.

Roxanne Brant

1
What Is Ministering To The Lord?

One of the main reasons for the "power failure" today in the Christian church is that Christians have failed to minister to the Lord. Biblically, the evidence is that our ministry to the Lord must come before our ministry to men if we are to be effective. Even after being filled with the Holy Spirit, if our priorities regarding these two types of ministry are reversed, we will be helpless and impotent before the heathen world.

We need to once again dig down into the springs of God's Life and bury ourselves in Him, the Source. We need to be caught up in the wonder of the Person of Jesus Christ of Nazareth, to know Him intimately and deeply. We will then find that our ministry Godward will urge us manward with a new freshness and power. Then we will not only talk of God's power but will also see it demonstrated.

Never has God so burned a truth into my being and so branded it upon my soul as the truth that our first ministry is to Him and not to men.

The revolution in my life began one day when the Holy Spirit gently began whispering to me, "Minister to the Lord. Minister to the Lord." For several days, this phrase kept coming through my mind. So I began to search the Scriptures.

I found that to serve the Lord, or to minister to the Lord, could be translated from some of the same Hebrew and Greek words (Hebrew—*sharath;* Greek—*diakoneo*).

There are many ways in which believers minister to (or serve) the Lord. We can minister to Him by ministering to those whom He loves. (See Matthew 25:40.) We can minister to Him by presenting Him with our tithes and offerings. We can minister to Him by offering Him our praise and worship.

Despite the numerous ways in which we can minister to God, I knew that the Holy Spirit was speaking about the latter way—about ministering to God in praise and worship.

It is amazing how often "ministering to the Lord" is mentioned in the Bible.

During the stay at Sinai while Israel was in the wilderness, "the Lord separated the tribe of Levi, to bear the ark of the covenant of the Lord, to stand before the Lord to minister unto Him, and to bless in His name" (Deuteronomy 10:8).

During the spiritually barren days before the rule of Israel's kings, when the word of the Lord was precious and there was no open vision, little Samuel "ministered unto the Lord before Eli" (I Samuel 2:18, 3:1).

When the temple was completed, during the reign of Solomon, the ark was brought from Zion into the most holy place.

"And it came to pass, when the priests were come out of the holy place . . . the trumpeters and singers were as one to make one sound to be heard in praising and thanking the Lord; and when they lifted up their voice with the trumpets and cymbals and instruments of musick, and praised the Lord, saying, For he is good; for his mercy endureth for ever: that then the house was filled with a cloud, even the house of the Lord; So that the priests could not stand to minister by reason of the cloud: for the glory of the Lord had filled the house of God" (II Chronicles 5:11-14).

Mary, the mother of Jesus, ministered to the Lord as she spoke forth the marvelous worship and praise of the Magnificat. (See Luke 1:46-55; cf. I Samuel 2:1-10)

Anna, the prophetess, who "spake of Him (Jesus) to all them that looked for redemption in Jerusalem," never left the Temple but "served (or ministered to) the Lord with fastings and prayers night and day" (Luke 2:36-38).

The leaders of the early church not only ministered to the Lord privately but came together publicly to fast and minister to the Lord. (Acts 13:1-3.)

Not only do we minister to the Lord here on earth, but millions in heavenly places minister to the Lord.

The Apostle John writes: *"And I beheld, and I heard the voice of many angels round about the throne and the beasts and the elders: and the number of them was ten thousand times ten thousand, and thousands of thousands; Saying with a loud voice, Worthy is the Lamb that was slain to receive power, and riches, and wisdom, and strength, and honour, and glory, and blessing. And every creature which is in heaven, and on the earth, and under the earth, and such as are in the sea, and all that are in them, heard I saying, Blessing, and honour, and glory, and power, be unto him that sitteth upon the throne, and unto the Lamb for ever and ever. And the four beasts said, Amen. And the four and twenty elders fell down and worshipped him that liveth for ever and ever"* (Revelation 5:11-14).

How numerous are the references in the Bible to ministering to the Lord! How important it is to understand God's loving design for us as we learn to minister to Him now and equip ourselves for that same ministry for eternity!

Understanding God's Purposes

Before we can understand our responsibility of ministering to the Lord and see it in perspective, we must understand God's purposes from the beginning of time and even before creation.

It is important to note that God has sovereignly declared that He made all things, including man, for Himself, that is, for His pleasure and for His glory.

"For by him were all things created, that are in heaven, and that are in earth . . . all things were created by him, and for him: And he is before all things, and by him all things consist" (Colossians 1:16-17).

In Revelation 4:8-11, the Apostle John describes the four living creatures who worship God day and night saying, "Holy, holy, holy Lord God Almighty, which was, and is, and is to come." He tells of the twenty-four elders who worship God by falling down before Him and casting their crowns before His throne. They are saying, "Thou art worthy, O Lord, to receive glory and honor and power: for thou hast created all things, and for thy pleasure they are and were created."

God, in speaking about each one of us, says in Isaiah 43:7, "for I have created him for my glory, I have formed him; yea, I have made him." Later on in the same chapter He sovereignly declares, "This people have I formed for myself; they shall shew forth my praise" (verse 21).

You are made for God—for His pleasure and to praise and worship Him forever. God saved you first of all for Himself. But **He wants you for yourself**—not just so that you can do something for Him. **He saved you because He loved you and because He wanted you.**

Man is created for God. God loves Jesus so much that He wants to fill the universe with a people who are formed in Jesus' image. (Romans 8:29.) He wants a people who will minister to Him for eternity and with whom He can share Himself.

As with Israel, so it is with us. God chooses us because He loves us and not because of any special virtue in us. Moses told Israel, "The Lord did not set his love upon you, nor choose you, because ye were more in number than any people; for ye were the fewest of all people: But because the Lord loved you . . ." (Deuteronomy 7:7-8).

Why do you love God? Because He has given you gifts, prospered you, healed you, and poured His blessings upon you? That's partially acceptable, but not completely. For to many people, their religion is the coin that purchases the benefits of God.

Yet, isn't there a higher form of love?

When we begin to see who He is and appreciate His person, don't we begin to love Him for Himself also?

We don't love our children because of their abilities. We love them for themselves, for who they are. Our wives, our husbands, our fathers and mothers—we are grateful for what they have done for us, but we love them for who they are.

We love Him because of who He is, and because He first loved us. God longs for our love and ministry to Him; but too often, we have only gone to Him to receive things from Him and to ask favors of Him.

How much this reminds me of a story I heard somewhere about President Lincoln and a very elderly lady who made an appointment to see him one afternoon.

As she entered the President's office, he arose, seated her and asked, "How may I be of service to you, madame?"

The little lady said, "Mr. President, I know you are a busy man. I have not come to ask you for anything. I simply came to bring you this box of cookies for I heard that you enjoy them so much."

A silence followed in which tears overflowed the eyes of the President. Finally, he raised his head and spoke to the little woman. "Madame, I thank you for your thoughtful gift. I am greatly moved by it. Since I have been the President of this country, thousands of people have come into this office asking for favors and demanding things from me. You are the first person who has ever entered these premises asking no favor, and indeed, bring a gift for me. I thank you from the bottom of my heart."

In the same way, God longs for us to come to Him for Himself, instead of simply for what He can give us. He has formed us for Himself, and it is we who are to present ourselves to Him and offer Him our worship.

The Bible says that we are God's inheritance. "For the Lord's portion is his people; Jacob is the lot of his inheritance" (Deuteronomy 32:9). God has an inheritance in the saints!

Paul prayed without ceasing for the church he established. To the church at Ephesus he wrote: *"I have never stopped thanking God for you. I pray for you constantly, asking God, the glorious Father of our Lord Jesus Christ, to give you wisdom to see clearly and really understand who Christ is and all that he has done for you. I pray that your hearts will be flooded with light so that you can see something of the future he has called you to share. I want you to realize that God has been made rich because we who are Christ's have been given to him"* (Ephesians 1:16-18 *The Living Bible*).

Think of it! The Bible says that, "God has been made rich because we who are Christ's have been given to Him!"

He wants us for ourselves. God is interested in a love relationship with us!

How wrong the church has been so often to teach new Christians that we are saved to serve God. NO! We are saved primarily because He wants us for Himself. That is why He has "loved back our lives from the pit of destruction and cast all our sins behind His back" (Isaiah 38:17, *The Amplified Bible*).

God isn't in the business of saving people because He needs a large number of servants to win the world for Christ, or because without us He might lose the battle against the devil. Yet, many Christians believe that they are working for a semi-impotent God who needs their help and expects them to repay Him for all His goodness to them.

The Bible never once tells us to do anything FOR God. It tells us that in His love and grace, God chose to INVOLVE us in what He is doing. We can work WITH Him and allow Him to work THROUGH us.

God could have evangelized this world with a group of angels, but He chose to give us the pleasure and privilege of working together with Him to accomplish that end.

Unfortunately, because the church so often teaches that we are here first to serve God, we have an abundance of guilt-laden Marthas, who are cumbered about with much anxious serving. And there is a dearth of worship-oriented Marys, who have entered into the rich love relationship with God, out of which the burden for human need so naturally springs.

How simply our Lord's words show us His priority.

"Now it came to pass, as they went, that he entered into a certain village: and a certain woman named Martha received him into her house.

"And she had a sister called Mary, which also sat at Jesus' feet, and heard his word.

"But Martha was cumbered about much serving, and came to him, and said, Lord, dost thou not care that my sister hath left me to serve alone? bid her therefore that she help me.

"And Jesus answered and said unto her, Martha, Martha, thou art careful and troubled about many things.

"But one thing is needful: and Mary hath chosen that good part, which shall not be taken away from her" (Luke 10:38-42).

Jesus did not rebuke Martha's serving but her overconcern and anxious preoccupation with "things" more than with God. **Service which is born of a love relationship is not anxious, but meaningful and joy-filled.**

Our first obligation in our relationship to God is LOVE. Yet, we have centered our attention on ministries, gifts, order, different types of programs and services, and so forth. We have centered our attention on everything except Him. We can see the results of that misdirected attention in our church life today.

God speaks to us as He spoke to Israel saying, "My people have committed two evils: they have forsaken me the fountain of living waters, and hewed them out cisterns, broken cisterns, that can hold no water" (Jeremiah 2:13).

God amazed me several years ago when He showed me that many people involved in the charismatic movement had turned to "broken cisterns" instead of to Him. Because of the abundant outpouring of good teaching, people were purchasing tapes and books and attending seminars to learn more about God's power and His ways and what He was doing on the earth at that time. Tapes and books and conferences are good. But God showed me that His people were substituting them for their time for waiting upon Him.

Sometimes it is so easy to hear from others ABOUT God and what He is doing that we don't bother to come TO Him to find out what He wants to say to us. We don't bother to commune with Him and receive that life-giving word from God ourselves. IF THIS HAPPENS, then those tapes, books and conferences become broken cisterns. And the water from cisterns is never as fresh and pure as the water from God's moving, flowing, life-giving fountain.

The danger today is that we will merely center on the *tree of knowledge* and forget the *tree of life;* that we will be satisfied with knowledge and forget the life of God: that we will be satisfied with the words of men and forget our need for the life-giving words of God.

So many of us need to turn to God and let Him, the Fountain of Life-giving Waters, flow through us, cleanse us, and fill us daily with His life. We need to have God, by His Spirit, reveal things to us in a fresh way. We need to go to God for Himself and for a *Living Word.*

The Pharisees knew what God had said. They had built cisterns. They were opaque and deaf to what God was saying in their time, simply because they had forsaken Him and built little cisterns AROUND His Words. **We need to know what God has said and what He is saying today**. When we, like the Pharisees of old, are not in God's life-giving flow, then our spiritual senses tend to become dulled and deadened. Then we have little or no spiritual perception or discernment.

God cries to us, "Come unto *Me.*" He has brought us out of the Egypt of darkness and bondage and given us an inheritance in His Kingdom. But we, like Israel, have turned from Him to idols, even religious idols. For the worship of traditions, programs, orders, and the like, that we put over Him in importance, are idols. If we, like Israel, put a greater emphasis on the importance of the form than the life, then we become legalistic, sectarian, and eventually dead. We are clinging to the remnant of a form while the life of God moves on elsewhere to those who will put Him first. Like Israel, will we return to the bondage of Egypt because we won't put God first and love Him first?

"When Israel was a child I loved him as a son and brought him out of Egypt. But the more I called to him, the more he rebelled, sacrificing to Baal and burning incense to idols. I trained him from infancy, I taught him to walk, I held him in my arms. But he doesn't know or even care that it was I who raised him" (Hosea 11:1-5 *The Living Bible*).

In our human relationships, as in our relationship to God, our first obligation is LOVE. Success outside the home does not make up for a lack of love in the home. God's order in a home means nothing if there is no love and life of Christ in that home.

So many people will do any amount of service rather than love. Unfortuantely, we are by nature doers like Martha, instead of lovers and worshipers, like Mary. God is seeking those who will love Him enough to come and be with Him and worship Him. He does not seek workers but he seeks worshipers. He seeks those who will "worship Him in spirit and in truth" (John 4:23-24).

Only after that love relationship has been rightly established and all has been centered upon Him, can He safely send us out to work with Him.

Man is made for God. But God is also in a sense made for man. God made man so that He could relate to man. In other words, God wants to give Himself to us. He created us not only that we might give ourselves to Him, but that He might also give Himself to us.

It was God who came down to walk with Adam and Eve in the garden. (Genesis 3:8.)

He created us with the capacity to receive Him. How often it happens that when we worship God, He comes to us. We see it in the Scriptures and also in our experience: worship brings us into God's presence and brings God's presence into us. As we worship God, He gives Himself to us.

In II Chronicles 5, it is interesting to note that when the temple of Solomon was finished, the elders of Israel gathered. The ark was brought into the temple by the Levites—but the glory of God did not come down. There were innumerable sacrifices offered—but the glory of God did not come down.

It was not until the trumpeters and singers "were as one, to make one sound to be heard in praising and thanking the Lord," that the glory of God came down. For "then the house was filled with a cloud, even the house of the Lord; So that the priests could not stand to minister by reason of the cloud: for the glory of the Lord had filled the house of God" (II Chronicles 5:13-14).

It was not when they built the temple. It was not when they offered sacrefices. It was when they praised and worshiped God that the glory of the Lord came down.

I think that when God hears His people worshiping Him and giving themselves to Him, He is moved and says within Himself, "I want to go down and hear my people worship and adore Me. They are giving themselves to Me and I am going to give myself to them." It is when we worship Him that He comes to us. For worship brings us into His presence and brings His presence into us.

Wherever we hold healing services, I teach the people how to minister to the Lord. I know that it is as we minister to Him that He will turn and minister to us and through us and a life-flow will be established. As we worship God, He heals people everywhere, sovereignly falling upon them. But the most wonderful thing is the sense of His presence.

About one time in every three or four meetings, the sense of His presence becomes so strong that all activity is suspended and we wait in the supercharged silence to see what He will do. Sometimes we wait five minutes, sometimes more, scarcely breathing and aware only of the beating of our hearts and of the closeness of our communion with the Almighty as He impresses himself upon us.

Once, as we worshiped Him and sang, "He Touched Me," half of the people present at the service heard the angels singing along with us. I didn't hear them myself so I asked what they sounded like. The people said that the choir of angelic voices was pitched at least an octave above a high soprano range and sounded like a hundred, clear, rich bells.

At another service, as we worshiped the Lord, my eyes were opened for a moment and I saw a huge angel standing right in front of the pulpit. He was facing the people so that his back was toward me. I saw that he was very powerfully built, about ten feet tall, and dressed in white with a Greek Key design embroidered in gold on his garment. For a moment I was stupified. God's presence flooded the sanctuary.

Then I realized why such a powerful angel was present. I began to smell a beautiful incense and feel God's presence in a special way. Minutes passed as we all became still in His presence. The incense pervaded the sanctuary and every person smelled it. Many fell on their knees, others wept, and others just quietly worshiped God—communing with Him in the stillness of His presence.

It is as we worship Him that He comes to us and gives Himself to us that we might receive Him in a fresh and fuller way. He created us to minister to Him. We were formed for His glory and to offer Him our praise and worship and to commune with Him; that in so doing, He might give himself to us.

When God brought the four million Hebrews out of Egypt, it is significant to note that He planned in His heart to make them all priests. He did not want only one priestly tribe, the tribe of Levi. He wanted to make the whole nation a "kingdom of priests and a holy nation" unto Him. That was His purpose.

God commanded Moses, *"Thus shalt thou say to the house of Jacob, and tell the children of Israel; Ye have seen what I did unto the Egyptians, and how I bare you on eagles' wings, and brought you unto myself. Now therefore, if ye will obey my voice indeed, and keep my covenant, then ye shall be a peculiar treasure unto me above all people: for all the earth is mine: And ye shall be unto me a kingdom of priests, and an holy nation"* (Exodus 19:3-6).

God brought the children of Israel unto Himself. He promised them that if they would fulfill two conditions—obey His voice, and keep His covenant— that they would be unto Him a peculiar (special) people above all the people on the earth, a kingdom of priests and a holy nation. God was saying to them, "I want to make every one of you a priest unto Me. I want a nation of priests. All you have to do is obey My voice and keep My covenant."

The people said, "All the words which the Lord hath said will we do" (Exodus 24:3). But it wasn't long before they were worshiping a molten calf (one of the old gods they worshiped in Egypt) and sitting down to eat and drink and rising up to play. (Exodus 32.)

Before Moses came down from Mount Sinai with the tables of the Law in his hand, the people had already broken God's covenant and disobeyed His voice. When Moses' anger "waxed hot" and he cast down and broke the tablets of the Law, he was only doing outwardly, in breaking the tablets, what the people *had already done inwardly*, in breaking the law of God in their hearts and actions.

The people violated both of the conditions God had set up. He could not make them a kingdom of priests. Not only did they disobey His voice, they "entreated that the word should not be spoken to them any more, for they could not endure that which was commanded" (Hebrews 12:19-20).

God's only alternative then was to make the tribe of Levi priests unto Him.

"At that time the Lord separated the tribe of Levi, to bear the ark of the covenant of the Lord, to stand before the Lord to minister unto Him, and to bless in his name unto this day. Wherefore Levi hath no part nor inheritance with his brethren; the Lord is his inheritance, according as the Lord thy God promised him" (Deuteronomy 10:8-9).

God wanted to do with all Israel what He finally had to end up doing with only one tribe. God wanted to make all Israel priests unto Him: to bear the ark of the covenant of the Lord, that is, to bear the PRESENCE OF GOD; to stand before the Lord to minister unto Him and bless His name. THE LORD,

HIMSELF, WOULD BE THEIR INHERITANCE. They would glory in Him.

Don't you see what He wanted then, and what He wants today? His purposes for the Levites were His original purposes for all of Israel. These are also His purposes for us today. God wants a people for himself who will minister to Him and a people to whom He can give himself.

God [through Christ] has accomplished His purpose. Peter writes that we who are Christians have been made ". . . an holy priesthood, to offer up spiritual sacrifices, acceptable to God by Jesus Christ" (I Peter 2:5). He continues, "But ye are a chosen generation, a royal priesthood, an holy nation, a peculiar (special) people; that ye should shew forth the praises of him who hath called you out of darkness into his marvellous light" (I Peter 2:9).

We are priests of the King!

God's purpose has been accomplished in Christ. Through Jesus, each believer becomes a priest unto God, to bear His presence and to stand before Him to minister to Him and bless His name. In turn, God gives Himself to us. He becomes our inheritance! How glorious!

Praise, Worship, and Communion

When we speak of ministering to the Lord, we speak primarily of three things: *praise, worship,* and *communion.*

As priests unto God, we no longer offer the bloody sacrifices of the Old Testament. We offer the spiritual sacrifices of the New Testament.

Hebrews 13:15 tells us to, "offer the sacrifice of praise to God continually, that is, the fruit of our lips giving thanks to his name."

Praise, worship and communion are involved in our ministry to the Lord. These are three very different things.

I think today, that the reason we have such an emphasis on praise and such an absence of worship is because people do not understand the difference between these two types of ministry. There are so many books written about praise, and so few about worship.

I would like to concentrate on our ministry to the Lord in worship, but it will be necessary to briefly discuss praise. Generally, the main difference between praise and worship is that **praise involves responding to God for what He has done** (mighty works, etc.), while **worship centers in who God is, in His person** (for example, "How Great Thou Art").

The word, "praise," comes from many different Hebrew and Greek roots. Some of these are translated as follows: praise, thanksgiving (Hebrew—*hillulim*); psalm (Hebrew—*tehillah*); confession (Hebrew—*todah*); courage, excellency (Greek—*arete*); glory (Greek—*doxa*); commendation (Greek—*epainos*); to bless, declare blessed (Hebrew—*barak*); to stretch out the hand, confess (Hebrew—*yadah*); to speak well of (Greek—*eulogeo*); to boast, praise (Hebrew—*halal*); to hymn (Greek—*humneo*).

Therefore, when you praise God you are blessing and commending and boasting of Him. At times you are offering thanksgiving, psalms, hymns and stretching out your hands before Him and glorifying Him by talking about His excellence, and so forth.

Everywhere, the Bible commands us to praise the Lord. In fact it says, "Let everything that hath breath praise the Lord" (Psalm 150:6).

As we minister to Him, we "enter into His gates with thanksgiving, and into His courts with praise." We are to be "thankful unto Him and bless His name" (Psalm 100:4).

I believe that we can enter into His gates with thanksgiving and into His courts with praise; but if we wish to prostrate ourselves right at His feet, *we have to know how to WORSHIP Him.*

I said that the basic difference is that praise centers upon what God has done and worship centers upon who He is. You know, we can thank and praise and adore human beings, as well as God Almighty. But we cannot worship any human being. We can worship only God. Why? Because only God is worthy.

The word, "worship," comes from an old Anglo-Saxon word, *weorth-scipe.* During the passage of years it became *worth-ship*. (They used to call the old English lords, your worth-ship.) This word has now become worship.

To worship means "to ascribe worth." That is why we read in Revelation 4:11, that God is "worthy . . . to receive glory and honour and power." He created all things. He created them for His pleasure.

It is interesting to note that God is worthy *to receive*.

So often we are only interested in what we can receive from Him for ourselves. David didn't only say, "Bless me O Lord." He also said, "Bless the Lord, O my soul" (Psalm 103:1).

In worship we adore Him for WHO He is rather than merely for WHAT HE HAS DONE.

Another clue to the meaning of worship is to be found in Genesis 22, where we see it first used in the Bible. When God tested Abraham by telling him to go and offer up Isaac as a burnt offering in the land of Moriah, Abraham heard God's command and arose to obey it. On the third day of his journey, Abraham saw the place of sacrifice afar off. He said to the men who accompanied him, "Abide ye here with the ass; and I and the lad will go yonder and worship" (Genesis 22:1-5). **We see here that worship involves giving something to God.**

The Bible tells us, *"Give unto the Lord the glory due unto His name: bring an offering and come before*

Him: worship the Lord in the beauty of holiness" (I Chronicles 16:29).

When the wise men came from the east to Jerusalem to worship Jesus, they came "into the house and they saw the young child with Mary his mother, and fell down, and worshipped him: and when they had opened their treasures, they presented unto him gifts; gold, and frankincense, and myrrh" (Matthew 2:11).

Worship involves giving something to God because He is worthy.

Several years ago, something very supernatural and unforgettable occurred that left a deep impression on me. It taught me that my first ministry is to the Lord and that to praise Him without worshiping Him is not enough. The Lord, Himself, came and showed me these things. He taught me the difference between praise and worship.

It happened one evening while I was ministering in a charismatic Presbyterian church. The songleader had led the congreation for about twenty minutes. They were singing the usual songs of praise and thanksgiving to God for healing, prospering and saving people—songs such as, "Amazing Grace," "He Touched Me," "Blessed Assurance," and others.

When it was time to speak, the minister arose and began to introduce me. Suddenly, to the right of the minister I saw Jesus. He was standing there with the loneliest expression I have ever seen on any face. His soft brown eyes overflowed with tears which began to pour down His cheeks and drop silently at His feet. There was no noise, no sobbing, and no movement of anything but the tears as they silently streamed down His face and dropped to the floor. The sense of His loneliness filled my being. I wanted to comfort Him. How lonely He was, even in the midst of all His people.

He disappeared as suddenly as He had appeared. I knew in an instant why He had been weeping. He was lonely because, in spite of all our self-centered singing ABOUT Him, He Himself was completely ignored. No wonder He wept. Of course He was lonely.

My mind was so filled with what I had seen, that when I came to the realization that I had just been introduced to the congregation, I seemed unable to speak. I arose and turned to them, still choking down the sobs which filled me. I managed to speak several words. All I could say was, "Now, let's worship Jesus."

Immediately it seemed as if the Holy Spirit flooded the sanctuary and began to move like a soft wind through a giant, divine harp.

For the next fifteen to twenty minutes everyone in the congregation began singing in the Spirit such exquisitely beautiful arrangements as no human mind could conceive.

The Holy Spirit was using our bodies as instruments for the expression of His own worship to the Lord Jesus Christ. He had heard our feeble attempts to praise Jesus. Now He filled our vocal apparatus with his own perfect, holy songs of worship.

How indispensable we were to each other, the Spirit and each of us! I remember, particularly, how a man on one side of the auditorium and a woman on the other kept singing cascades of prophetic worship up and down the scale in perfect harmony as they worshiped the Lord in the Spirit. It sounded as if passages out of the book of Revelation were being brought to life.

As the people continued to worship Jesus, I became aware of something happening within me. The intense loneliness which I had previously experienced slowly began leaving me. It was replaced by a feeling of satisfaction and joy. Although I could no longer see Jesus, the Holy Spirit let me know that He also was feeling the same thing. I knew that the loneliness was leaving Him as the people continued to minister to Him. I knew that He was feeling satisfaction and joy from their worship.

There was such a glorious, festal presence of the Holy Spirit that we felt as if we were in a heavenly banquet and that any minute we could put our hand on the arm of the King of kings and march right up the aisle with Him.

After some time, the Holy Spirit gradually lifted His hand from us. I knew it was time for the message. Again, Jesus spoke very clearly to me and said, "You have ministered to me, so now I will minister to you." Then I arose and gave a message on *"Ministering to the Lord."*

I share this with you because I am convinced that Jesus is all too frequently lonely at the services we claim to hold in His name. So many services are centered only in praise, and ignore His presence with us. This is not enough. We also need services which are centered in worship, a worship in which the believer is caught up in the present reality of God's person, in the reality of who He is.

We have talked about praise and worship. **We need to say something about communion with God, where we go BEYOND the altar of incense, into the Holy of Holies where the ark of His PRESENCE is.**

When someone is born again, he is quickened and becomes alive in his spirit. He begins to commune with God in this very deepest place of his innermost being. (I John 1:1-3.) The human spirit (and not the mind) is the place where God communes with us as we quietly wait upon Him. It is in our spirit where He unfolds His revelations to us as we are capable of receiving them through His Spirit and His Word.

Let me mention here that there are no "new revelations" such as some might teach; but just the good, solid, Biblical truths made alive and fresh to us by the Holy Spirit. Don't forget that everything must be in line with God's objective standard of truth, the written Word of God.

As we commune with the Lord, a flow of life is established.

Isaiah writes, *"They that wait upon the Lord shall renew their strength; they shall mount up with wings as eagles; they shall run and not be weary; and they shall walk, and not faint"* (Isaiah 40:31).

As we wait upon the Lord, there is a change or passing on of strength. If we wait upon the Lord, we shall exchange our **WEAKNESS** for God's STRENGTH. (*Exchange* is a better translation of the Hebrew word, *chalaph* meaning "to change, to pass on," than *renew* as used in this passage.)

As we wait upon the Lord and commune with Him, we begin to absorb some of His strength. He impressed himself and His mind upon us. That is why the psalmist says, "My soul, wait thou only upon God; for my expectation is from Him" (Psalm 62:5). Also, "I wait for the Lord, my soul doth wait, and in His word do I hope. My soul waiteth for the Lord more than they that watch for the morning" (Psalm 130:5-6).

We need to learn to minister to the Lord in praise, worship and communion. It is as we praise Him and thank Him for His goodness to us that we can so easily move into worship—just worshiping Him for who He is. It is then, as we worship Him, that the flow of worship moves us into His presence (right before the throne of God Almighty). His presence then moves into us in a way in which we FEEL it, and communion is established.

Then God's heart is stirred. He begins to move upon us, pouring His blessings, His presence, revelations and heavenly goodness into our spirits as we are simply still and wait upon Him, letting Him minister to us.

How simply each facet of ministering to the Lord fits together! How exciting it is to let the Holy Spirit move through us to minister to the Lord of the whole universe!

Now that we have talked about what ministering to the Lord is, and some of the concepts and content involved in that ministry, let's look at the priority the Bible places on it.

2
Our First Ministry

The Bible is clear that the first obligation of a Christian is ministry to the Lord. God places the priority on ministry to himself.

Even in a corporate sense, how clear it is when one reads the Scriptures that the reason the Church exists is **first,** *to minister to the Lord;* **second,** *to minister to the saints;* **third,** *to minister to the world.*

The very first reason for our being baptized in the Spirit is not to witness to men but to worship the Lord. When we put this first, the other essentials of the Christian life all fall into place. It is for this reason that the Spirit gives believers a supernatural language with which to worship God acceptably. We cannot rightly perform our first ministry to Him without the ability to pray in the Spirit.

Whenever God does something the first time, it is well for us to look closely at the details.

For example, in the first chapter of the book of Genesis, we see that when God created the heavens and earth, He *first* moved by His Spirit and *then* spoke the word and all things came into being.

First, the Spirit moves and second, God's Word comes forth. God moves according to that same pattern today.

It is well that we read carefully the first chapter of Genesis. We need to learn that valuable lesson: the Holy Spirit and the Word ALWAYS work together.

In Acts chapter two, we see another one of God's patterns. Pentecost is the record of the first time that the Holy Spirit was poured out upon ALL flesh (not just upon prophets, priests, and kings). ALL FLESH includes men, women and children, those who were just ordinary laborers, housewives, and so forth.

As we study closely how God worked when the Holy Spirit first came upon all flesh, we see that He *first* used men and women to utter the praises of God. He *then* used Peter to preach the gospel to several thousand people and convert them. Worship to God came first. Witness to men followed.

Through the New Testament, the Scriptures bear witness of this order. We will find that this is the way the Holy Spirit moves in our lives today if we will but follow His guidance.

At Pentecost, the new Christians spoke in other tongues (or supernaturally given languages) as the Spirit gave them utterance. All of the dispersed Jews who came heard this, and many understood the beautiful languages which were being spoken. They heard the new Christians speak the wonderful works of God in languages that were given by the Holy Spirit.

"And when the day of Pentecost was fully come, they were all with one accord in one place.

"And suddenly there came a sound from heaven as of a rushing mighty wind, and it filled all the house where they were sitting.

"And there appeared unto them cloven tongues like as of fire, and it sat upon each of them.

"And they were all filled with the Holy Ghost, and began to speak with other tongues, as the Spirit gave them utterance" (Acts 2:1-4).

"And how hear we every man in our own tongue, wherein we were born?" (verse 8).

". . . we do hear them speak in our tongues the wonderful works of God" (verse 11).

The *first* thing that the Holy Spirit did when He came upon the early Christians was to speak through them the praises of God. The *second* thing the Holy Spirit did was to move Peter to preach an evangelistic sermon which converted about three thousand people. (Acts 2:41.)

The Scripture tells us then, that the first reason we are baptized in the Holy Spirit is to enable us to minister to God and out of that ministry to Him the burden for evangelism comes.

In order to effectively worship God in Spirit and in truth, we need the supernatural enabling called the baptism with the Holy Spirit.

The first thing that happens to us when we are filled with the Holy Spirit is that we are given a supernatural language from God. Our hearts turn more completely to God, to whom we were already reconciled in Jesus Christ when we were born again. Now we draw closer to Him. We see an expansion of Him. We get a clearer revelation of Him. We move into another dimension.

Seeing God in this manner, we want to worship Him in the language He has given. There is no other normal response from a believer to his God, after he has been baptized in the Holy Spirit, except to worship Him. Human words are too limited. They cannot contain the flood of worship that moves up through the soul. Therefore, God has given us an unlimited language, a language that is supernatural, a gift from Him.

So many people ask me, "Why do I need to pray in tongues?"

I simply tell them that if they do not accept this gift of tongues from God, then they cannot responsibly and effectively perform their first ministry, which is their ministry to Him.

So many people tell God that they want all of the spiritual gifts *except* tongues.

They don't trust God to give them good gifts!

They are like a man who walks into a shoe store and buys a pair of shoes but says to the shoe clerk, "I will not take that pair of shoes home unless you cut out the tongues." How silly!

Trust God and take the whole package of gifts for His glory and the benefit of others.

How wonderful it is to be able to worship God without limitation; to get caught up in the glory and wonder of the person of Christ; and to come to know Him more intimately and deeply than is possible in any other way.

And when tribulations come which would overthrow the strongest saint, one continues to worship because he is empowered by the Spirit.

The Bible clearly shows us that our first ministry is to the Lord and our second (and resultant) ministry is to men.

In the second chapter of his first letter, Peter likens Christians to living stones. These are not ordinary stones; they are alive. At first glance, that seems to be a very odd way to describe a believer in Jesus Christ. But when we remember that Christ is likened to a rock, and we who believe receive His rock nature, then we can begin to understand why Peter uses the metaphor of living stones.

"Ye also, as lively (living) *stones, are built up a spiritual house, an holy priesthood, to offer up spiritual sacrifices, acceptable to God by Jesus Christ . . .*

"But ye are a chosen generation, a royal priesthood, an holy nation, a peculiar (treasured) *people; that ye should shew forth the praises of him who hath called you out of darkness into his marvellous light"* (I Peter 2:5,9).

Peter states that every believer is built into a spiritual house. We fit together like living, singing stones. Thus, the whole house grows to the accompaniment of spiritual sacrifices, the sacrifices of praise and worship. We are continually to minister to the Lord as a holy priesthood which offers the sacrifices of praise and worship to God without ceasing.

How often we approach God and ask Him only for what we can get. "God give me a message for your people. Heal my friends. Provide for my needs. Help this missionary," and so forth.

But God is trying to make us understand something. He is saying to us, "If you would only worship Me, if you would only come and minister to Me, then every prayer that I put into your heart to pray would be answered. Everything else will follow if you will only come and worship Me first; if you will only come and seek Me, the One who is above."

God has created, shaped and filled us that we might be vessels overflowing with praise to Him alone, pouring out a ministry of worship to Him that will stretch and crescendo into the limitless ages of eternity.

We are temples. The Bible says that our bodies are the temples of the Holy Spirit. You know what occurred in the temple—*praise* and *worship*, hours of praise and worship.

When we are filled with the Holy Spirit, hours of praise and worship should be poured out to God upon the altars of our hearts. And don't forget, the fire on the altar of the tabernacle in the Old Testament never went out, night or day—neither does the fire of the Holy Spirit in your heart. He burns continually, inspiring you to praise and worship God without ceasing, inspiring you to minister to Him.

That means that as priests unto God we minister to Him always. For example, at seven o'clock in the morning, when you men are shaving, offer up some spiritual sacrifices to God, some praise and worship to Him.

At that same time, when you ladies are turning the eggs over in the frying pan, offer up some spiritual sacrifices to God.

Twenty-four hours a day, whether you are awake or asleep, the Holy Spirit is alive and burning in you. He never goes to sleep. He can use you to minister to the Lord twenty-four hours a day, if He wills it and you allow Him to.

These are the days of restoration, that is, restoration of the truth.

Do you remember what the governor of the feast said to the bridegroom of the marriage feast where Jesus changed the water into wine? He said, "You have kept the good wine until the last; but most men set forth the good wine in the beginning of the feast."

We know that the wine at the end of the feast was best because Jesus miraculously made it. And the best wine in terms of the best teaching from the Bible is still to come today. One of these truths which He is restoring to the Church today is the truth that our first ministry is to Him.

I believe it is ridiculous for us to think that we can effectively minister to men without first learning how to minister to God. It is our ministry to God that urges us manward with an effectiveness and power that we so desperately need today. The baptism in the Holy Spirit is only the potential for that power. As we minister to the Lord and soak ourselves in Him, we come to the place where *He is our reward.* Not a ministry, not things, not healings or financial prosperity, but the Lord himself is our reward! He is our life, our everything.

So many people use their religion as a coin that purchases the benefits of God. How atrocious! God forgive us. They use their ministries to glorify themselves, and their energies to do the work of the Lord. How horrible!

If we would only do what God commanded, everything else would fall into place. And He would get all the glory.

He said, "*Seek ye first the kingdom of God, and his righteousness; and all these things shall be added unto you*" (Matthew 6:33).

We find that God speaks, answers prayers, and blesses us with His presence much more when we minister to Him than when we merely petition Him.

Let me give you an example. You gentlemen know that if you have a little six-year-old daughter, she may run to you when you come home from work. She'll climb up on your lap, put her little arms around your neck and give you a hug. Then she'll say, "Daddy, I saw a big lollipop over at the store. I would like it because it is lemon. It has a smile on it. It is so big it will last me for three months and it only costs two dollars. Daddy, would you give me two dollars so that I can buy that lollipop?"

Now gentlemen, if she simply asks you for that lollipop, you may give her two dollars to buy it or you may not. However, suppose your little daughter approaches you another way.

What if she runs into the living room, climbs up on your lap, puts her little arms around your neck, gives you a big hug and kiss and says, "Daddy, I am so glad that God gave me a Daddy like you. You are the best Daddy in the whole world. I love you so much."?

She does not need to ask you for anything. But I'll tell you how you will feel when she says that: you will feel like pulling your wallet out of your pocket and pouring it on that child. Why? Simply because she has moved your heart by the expression of her love.

So it is with us. When we come to the Lord for Himself and express our love for Him, His heart is moved. He pours out His blessing upon us and grants us our requests in a lavish way.

So often the Lord of the work suffers while we are busy with the work of the Lord.

We have put our first ministry second. We really need to repent, because in doing that we have committed idolatry. We have exalted the institution above our Lord. We have exalted the traditions of men above the gospel. We have exalted the work of the Lord above the Lord Himself. We are busy doing this or that or something else.

What God is trying to say to us is, "Peace be still. Go somewhere and minister to Me. Then there will be no wasted efforts, no wasted words and all will be done in the power of My Spirit."

Some people find it hard to believe this, but every time I draw apart, He meets me. I mean every time. I don't care where it is, it only takes a few minutes before I am caught up in worship to Him.

This can happen to you too, if you cultivate your relationship with Him. It takes time and effort but certainly no one else is as worthy of your attention as the Living God.

Anna, the prophetess, spent much time ministering to the Lord and in communion with Him.

"And there was one Anna, a prophetess, the daughter of Phanuel, of the tribe of Aser: she was of a great age, and had lived with an husband seven years from her virginity; And she was a widow of about fourscore and four years, which departed not from the temple, but served God with fastings and prayers night and day" (Luke 2:36-37).

This passage says that Anna *served* God with fastings and prayers night and day. It can also be translated, Anna *ministered* to the Lord with fastings and prayers night and day.

I'll be honest, when I first became a Christian, I read that passage and decided that Anna *had* to minister to the Lord with fastings and prayers night and day because she was so old. I assumed that she did not have anything else to do. Or, she could not do anything practical, like bringing people to God because she was too aged and weak.

After I began to see that a Christian's first ministry is to the Lord, I saw that Anna was doing the most important thing, performing the most important ministry of all.

If we try to walk where we have not prayed, or try to work before we have worshiped God, then we will only be serving Him in our own power. And all that work will eventually be burned up.

"Now if any man build upon this foundation gold, silver, precious stones, wood, hay, stubble; Every man's work shall be made manifest: for the day shall declare it, because it shall be revealed by fire; and the fire shall try every man's work of what sort it is. If any man's work abide which he hath built thereupon, he shall receive a reward. If any man's work shall be burned, he shall suffer loss: but he himself shall be saved; yet so as by fire" (I Corinthians 3:12-15).

When Mary and Joseph brought the baby Jesus into the Temple, Anna knew exactly what was going on. She was in God's place at God's time, filled with the revelation of who Jesus was. She gave God thanks and ". . . spake of Him (Jesus) to all them that looked for redemption in Jerusalem" (Luke 2:38).

Many people would say that Anna was aware of God's purpose in Christ, and of who Christ was because she was a prophetess. Therefore, God would reveal His secrets to her because Amos 3:7 says, "Surely the Lord God will do nothing but he revealeth his secret unto his servants the prophets."

But I believe that God showed her His secrets not just because she was a prophetess, but because she waited upon Him and ministered to Him. **It was as she ministered to the Lord that He opened to her His plans.**

If we would minister to Him, He would unfold His secrets, His revelations, and His mysteries to us also.

Anna was not running around doing things in her own strength. She was waiting upon the Lord and resting in Him, letting the Holy Spirit move through her to minister to God. Anna was spiritual.

So much of our Christian work today is soulish. So much of it is out of touch with the Lord, because WE are out of touch with the Lord.

We are so often out of touch with the Lord because we presume upon God, because we go ahead of Him.

How often we run ahead of the Lord and do so many things that seem good to us. Yet the Lord has not commanded us to do them. We are like the false prophets who ran and yet God said, "I have not sent them."

We must learn to worship the Lord and wait in His presence until He commands us to move. We must learn that going and doing what God has not commanded is sin, even though we do "good things."

So many people have been so busy doing good things that they are kept from God's best for them. They are kept from His highest purposes in their lives. To go ahead of the Lord and presume that we can accomplish anything that will endure for His kingdom is sheer folly. God forgive us for this sin of presumption.

It is not until we minister to the Lord that we are empowered to move manward in an effective and enduring way. We must not presume to go ahead of the Lord and do what He has not required us to do. Neither should we rebel against the Lord and go our own separate ways. *We are to follow Him and walk with Him.* To presume upon Him and walk ahead of Him is as bad a sin as to rebel against Him and go our own separate ways.

Someone said that if the Holy Spirit was taken from the earth, eighty percent of the Christian work would go on as usual. If that were true, it would mean that eighty percent of what God's Church was doing would be involved in the sin of presuming upon God.

How glibly we cite the scripture, "Not by might nor by power, but by my spirit, saith the Lord of hosts" (Zechariah 4:6), and yet work before we have worshiped the Lord.

Our ministry to men must flow from our ministry to God if it is to be effective. Otherwise it will be done in the power of the soul and with the wrong motivation. In a sense, we can say that worship must come before work and that **intensive** worship leads to **extensive** worship (or ministry to men).

When we put work before worship, all that we do comes to little.

The flesh drives us. The carnal nature keeps urging, *DO, DO, DO.*

God never says that. He says, "Rest in Me. Wait upon me. Abide in Me. When the times comes, I will urge you manward in service."

There's a beautiful image in the Song of Solomon in which Jesus says to the Church, His Bride, "Thine eyes are like the fish pools of Heshbon" (Song of Solomon 7:4).

God has lots of rivers. He has lots of streams and oceans and crashing waterfalls, but He does not have many pools. He has lots of people who jump up and down and run around and do all kinds of things. There are not very many people to whom God can say, "Be still," and they will obey Him and rejoice in waiting upon Him.

What does a pool do? A pool reflects. The believer reflects Jesus Christ just as a pool in the natural realm reflects the sun. Do you want a true picture of the sun, of the mountains or the trees? Look into a very still, deep pool.

That is what God wants to make you and me — still, deep pools which reflect His own Son.

After He gets the mud out, He lines these pools with the stones of His Truth. He then pours in pure water, the Holy Spirit himself. Then there is a depth, a freshness, and a clarity which was never there before.

This is one of the results of our worshiping God, of our communion with Him. We learn to wait on the Lord and become still, deep, Christ-reflecting pools. As the pool awaits the reflection upon it, so we have to learn to wait upon the Lord until He makes His impression upon us.

We have all kinds of programs and gadgets to get Christians moving, working, giving, but nothing is really going to happen until the pool reflects the Lord. This kind of power never comes from doing, but from waiting upon Him.

I've gone through seminary and I know all the programs. I spent four years there. I know how many programs we have to get people into our churches, to get people working and serving, to get people giving. But they are not about to succeed unless God's wine is flowing.

When you want to get in touch with the God of power, you go into a room for several days, shut the door behind you and spend time alone with the Bible and God. When you tell God you are not going to come out of that room until you have all that He has for you in Jesus, God is going to move. He will see your persistence and the wine of God will flow through your life. People will come to hear you because you've been ministering to the Lord.

You will begin to see people really touched by the hand of the Savior, not by the message alone but by the person of the Spirit of God.

If you take a brand and hold it in the fire, it will get red hot. Begin to abide. Begin to read the Word. Begin to minister to Him. Start doing the basic, simple things that Jesus taught. He gave us our methods. He gave us our approach. It doesn't matter whether the listeners live in mansions or adobe huts, the approach is the same. **In to worship and out to serve!**

Being filled with praise and worship to the Lord should be a result of walking in the fullness of the Holy Spirit. Paul in the fifth chapter of Ephesians tells us that if we are walking continually in the fullness of the Holy Spirit, there will be three manifest results.

"And be not drunk with wine, wherein is excess; but be filled with the Spirit; Speaking to yourselves in psalms and hymns and spiritual songs, singing and making melody in your heart to the Lord; Giving thanks always for all things unto God and the Father in the name of our Lord Jesus Christ; Submitting yourselves one to another in the fear of God" (Ephesians 5:18-21).

Firstly, **we will praise and worship God** (verse 19). Secondly, **we will thank God for all things** (verse 20).

Thirdly, **we will submit ourselves one to another in the fear of God** (verse 21). These are the three basic results that we should look for in our lives as we walk in the fullness of the Holy Spirit.

How interesting that Paul writes that the *first* evidence of our walking in the fullness of the Holy Spirit is the outpouring of worship and praise which rises spontaneously from Spirit-filled hearts. We go to Jesus because we are drawn by His love.

The most wonderful thing about my life is not the miracles or the healing ministry, but the joyful privilege I have of ministering to my Father in heaven. It is the wonderful realization every minute of the day that I am a child of God, led and guided by the Holy Spirit and walking with the King of Kings.

The early church knew that its first ministry was to the Lord.

In Acts 13, we find that the leaders of the church at Antioch knew a powerful secret. They knew that it was as they ministered to God that He would minister to them and through them. They gathered together and were fasting and praying and ministering unto the Lord. They had a church to launch and a world to win for Christ. But they knew they could only do it in God's power.

"As they ministered to the Lord, and fasted, the Holy Ghost said, Separate me Barnabus and Saul for the work whereunto I have called them" (verse 2).

As they ministered to the Lord, God spoke and gave them His methods, His wisdom and His power to conquer the world.

So often we say, "Lord, do this for us. Lord, bless our efforts." This is never right. We should rather minister to the Lord, be filled with His power and become quiet pools upon which the Holy Spirit can imprint His sovereign will.

As the early Christian leaders gathered together, they ministered to the Lord, and the Spirit directed their work and empowered them to conquer the world.

The priority of ministering to the Lord is at the heart of the Old Testament priesthood as well as the New.

The Old Testament priests ministered to the Lord AND to the people. But FIRST of all, they ministered to the Lord.

In Ezekiel 44 there is a beautiful passage concerning the two types of ministry that we are to perform as a royal priesthood: (for as such we have incorporated within us both types of ministries) a ministry to the Lord and a ministry to the people. Both types of ministry are essential; the tragic error lies in our ministering to the people BEFORE we minister to the Lord.

Certain of the Levites had led Israel astray in the worship of idols because they put things before God. They became to preoccupied with the ministry to people that they slipped away from God. God became indignant.

"And the Levites that are gone away from me, when Israel went astray, which went astray away from me after their idols; they shall even bear their iniquity.

"Yet they shall be ministers in my sanctuary, having charge at the gates of the house, and ministering to the house: they shall slay the burnt offering and the sacrifice for the people, and they shall stand before them to minister unto them. . .

"And they shall not come near unto me, to do the office of a priest unto me, nor to come near to any of my holy things, in the most holy place: but they shall bear their shame, and their abominations which they have committed.

"But I will make them keepers of the charge of the house, for all the service thereof, and for all that shall be done therein.

"But the priests the Levites, the sons of Zadok, that kept the charge of my sanctuary when the children of Israel went astray from me, they shall come near to me to minister unto me, and they shall stand before me to offer unto me the fat and the blood, saith the Lord God" (Ezekiel 44:10-15).

It does not matter whether the idols are of wood and stone or of self-motivated service for the Lord, both are idolatry.

God said, "All right. They are still my Levites, but they must bear their sin. And the consequence of their sin is that while they shall still minister in my sanctuary and be in charge of the gates of the house, they shall minister ONLY TO THE HOUSE."

They will slay the burnt offering and all the sacrifices for the people. As a type, they represent those who bring people to Christ through His blood. They will make peace with God for the people. They will evangelize the lost.

BUT, God decreed, "They shall not come near to Me!" Think what this means. These Levites will still minister to the house, but they shall not enjoy a real sense of nearness to their God as His priests. They can do the work of the Lord, but they can never again minister to the Lord of the work.

For someone who knows what it means to minister to the Lord Himself, this must be the most terrible consequence to bear. This need happen to no one, however, for God had kept for Himself a righteous remnant.

The other priests mentioned in the scripture here are called the sons of Zadok (verse 15). And since Zadok means "righteous," and since Jesus Christ is the righteous One, how significantly these sons of Zadok represent those Christians to come who would put ministering to God first in their lives.

These sons of Zadok, this scripture says, kept faithfully the charge of the Lord's sanctuary when the other priests led the Israelites astray by putting other things first.

God says of these sons of Zadok, "They shall enter into my sanctuary, and they shall come near to my table to minister unto me, and they shall keep my charge" (verse 16).

God says that they will come near Him because they have ministered to Him alone and first of all. They alone will have the most precious ministry—the ministry unto the Lord.

Nothing should hinder us in our ministry to the Lord.

Let catastrophes come, let depression come, let recession come, let anything come, we must minister to Him first and without fail! Before lunch, before dinner, before breakfast, before anything, we must minister to Him first. Nothing must come in the way of that sacred time with Him. Let one thing interfere and you're going to lose your time of worship. Let one compromise come in and you'll suffer loss.

There is a man who has written many good books on the Bible. He spent six hours every day of his life studying the Bible.

I went to see him and asked, "How in the world do you do it?"

He said, "You just make time."

That was a simple and true statement. He spent over 100,000 hours of his life studying the Bible. He authored many commentaries on the Bible. All because he would not let anything stop him from coming apart to study the Bible.

That is exactly what we have to do. If we care enough we will make time. God keeps reminding us that He is a jealous God, and only the sons of Zadok, the faithful remnant who came to minister unto Him, were permitted to stand in His presence.

Ezekiel declares the Word of the Lord further, with a very significant admonition.

"And it shall come to pass, that when they enter in at the gates of the inner court, they shall be clothed with linen garments; and no wool shall come upon them, while they minister in the gates of the inner court, and within. They shall have linen bonnets upon their heads, and shall have linen breeches upon their loins; they shall not gird themselves with anything that causeth sweat" (Ezekiel 44:17-18).

He states that when the priests come to enter into the inner court, they must be clothed only in linen garments, and no wool may touch them while they minister in God's presence.

Our God is a jealous God, and we are His workmanship. Therefore, He will not contaminate His glory with our sweat.

But what does sweat represent?

The key is in a passage in the New Testament. "For ye see your calling, brethren, how that not many wise men after the flesh, not many mighty, not many noble, are called: But God hath chosen the foolish things of the world to confound the wise; and God hath chosen the weak things of the world to confound the things which are mighty; And base things of the world, and things which are despised, hath God chosen, yea, and things which are not, to bring to nought things that are: That no flesh should glory in his presence" (I Corinthians 1:26-29).

See how perfectly this parallels Ezekiel 44!

The priests shall wear linen bonnets, linen breeches, so that nothing will come into God's presence that causes sweat. Obviously the flesh sweats and not the spirit.

God is saying that He doesn't want any fleshly worship. No flesh shall glory in His presence.

God cannot use men and women who are naturally capable and self-reliant. He wants those who rely upon Him for everything they do. That way, God gets the glory and not man. All our education and training has to be put on the cross along with all our sins, so that no flesh shall be tempted to glory in itself, but that the Holy Spirit may be the sole wisdom for our lives.

Paul said the same thing about himself. "But what things were gain to me, those I counted loss for

Christ. Yea doubtless, and I count all things but loss for the excellency of the knowledge of Christ Jesus my Lord . . . I count them but dung that I may win Christ" (Philippians 3:7-8).

Nothing that causes sweat can come into God's presence. God is tired of fleshly service and worship and is actively seeking a people who will minister to Him in the power of the Spirit.

That is why Jesus told the Samaritan woman, "But the hour cometh, and now is, when the true worshippers shall worship the Father in spirit and in truth: for the Father seeketh such to worship him. God is a Spirit: and they that worship him must worship him in spirit and in truth" (John 4:23-24).

God is looking for a people to minister to Him, to worship Him in Spirit and in truth.

Our highest function is to minister to God. And that ministry must come before all other. Jesus taught this truth in a parable.

"But which of you, having a servant plowing or feeding cattle, will say unto him by and by, when he is come from the field, Go and sit down to meat?

"And will not rather say unto him, Make ready wherewith I may sup, and gird thyself, and serve me, till I have eaten and drunken; and afterward thou shalt eat and drink?

"Doth he thank that servant because he did the things that were commanded him? I trow not.

"So likewise ye, when ye shall have done all those things which are commanded you, say, We are unprofitable servants: we have done that which was our duty to do" (Luke 17:7-10).

We see that two types of work are mentioned by our Lord: (1) the work of plowing the field or feeding the cattle and (2) the work of serving the Master.

When we return from the busy workaday world, we are commanded to first minister to God, to meet His desires before we satisfy our own.

His command to us is, "Gird yourself and serve Me, till I have finished My dinner, and then you shall have yours."

This is not an accurate picture of many Christian lives. After a hectic day's work, we come home, watch the news or read the paper and sit down to eat with the family. After dinner, we play with the children and read them a Bible story before their bedtime. Then we tuck them into bed and say "goodnight" to them. This leaves us two or three hours of free time for work, leisure and conversation before we happily close our eyes for the night.

We have been satisfied, warmed and filled. Yet while we rest so comfortably, Jesus is still sitting at the dinner table, hungry.

He has not been warmed or fed. He has not been ministered to. His desires have not been satisfied. God forgive us! We need to repent.

He seeks a people who will worship Him. He is hungry for our worship and our praise. We need to repent and put Him first and gird ourselves to minister to Him.

We must learn to come to Him and say, "Lord, I've come for no other purpose than to worship You. I am very tired this evening, but before I go to bed tonight, Lord, I have come to minister to You."

And after we have put Him first and ministered to His full satisfaction, we still need to realize that "we are unprofitable servants for we have merely done that which was our duty to do."

We need to go to God in repentance. "Father, forgive me for neglecting You and thinking only of myself. I am truly sorry. I want to return to my first ministry, my ministry to You. But I need Your help. Help me to rise earlier and come apart to wait upon You. Help me when so many things seem to clamor for my time and attention, to put You first, no matter what the cost."

Worship comes before work. The Lord of the work comes before the work of the Lord. To have a fruitful outer-court ministry, we must put our inner-court ministry first. For it is as we minister to Him that He ministers to us and through us. If we seek first the kingdom of God, and His righteousness, all the things we need will be added unto us. (Matthew 6:33.)

Cultivate the presence of the Lord. Worship Him and come into His presence and let His presence come into you.

3
The Ways Of Ministering To The Lord

We learn how to minister to the Lord by studying in the Scriptures how God's people ministered to Him and by ministering to Him ourselves.

There are several insights into the nature of ministering to the Lord in Genesis 22 where the word *worship* is first mentioned in the Bible.

When God told Abraham to sacrifice his son, Isaac, Abraham believed God and obeyed His command. When he reached the place of sacrifice, he came apart from the group of men who accompanied him. He said to them, "Abide ye here with the ass; and I and the lad will go yonder and worship and come again to you" (Genesis 22:5).

First, we see that Abraham believed God. Like Abraham, **we need faith to worship God.**

The Bible says, ". . . without faith it is impossible to please Him, for he that cometh to God must believe that he is, and that He is a rewarder of them that diligently seek him" (Hebrews 11:6).

Only after you have been born again and entered into the kingdom of God do you present yourself before God, by faith, and become aware that He is indeed very near to you. Only then can you engage in worship through the instrumentality of the Holy Spirit.

Secondly, Abraham obeyed God's command and came apart to sacrifice or worship. **Obedience and worship are related.**

As we obey Him more and more completely and each area of our lives comes under His control, we begin to see more and more who He is. When we see God, we have no other reaction than to worship Him.

The Bible says that our sins separate us from God and hide His face from us so that He will not hear us. (Isaiah 59:2.) Sin keeps us from God, from feeling His presence and from worshiping Him. But if we repent of our sins and obey Him in all the minute details of life, then we have rich fellowship with Him, which in turn enriches us and our ministry to God.

Notice that Abraham prepared to worship or sacrifice and came apart from the people who accompanied Him to worship the Lord.

We must prepare ourselves to worship the Lord. We cannot turn the television off one minute and worship the Lord the next minute. We must come apart from noisy, bustling people and situations and still our minds in preparation for worship. We need a place where, individually or collectively, our minds and spirits can be centered on God without distraction.

Abraham came apart to offer up Isaac to God and he called it worship. To worship means to give something to God, for He is worthy to receive "power, and riches, and wisdom, and strength and honor, and glory, and blessing" (Revelation 5:12).

God blessed a previously barren Hannah with the child for which she had prayed. She named him Samuel and brought him to give him to the Lord in Shiloh as she had promised.

She said, *"For this child I prayed; and the Lord hath given me my petition which I asked of him: Therefore also I have lent him to the Lord; as long as he liveth he shall be lent to the Lord. And* (they) *worshiped the Lord there"* (I Samuel 1:27-28).

Hannah said, "The Lord has given to me . . . I have given to the Lord." And the text says that (they) worshiped the Lord there.

The key to worship is giving something to God.

Worship is tied in with sacrifice.

After Paul and Silas were beaten with many stripes and cast into prison for the sake of the gospel, they prayed and sang praises to God. (Acts 16:25.) Their worship was a sacrifice pleasing to God.

When Job was informed that all of his children had been killed, "he arose, and rent his mantle, and shaved his head, and fell down upon the ground and worshiped" (Job 1:20). That worship involved sacrifice!

The Bible tells us in Romans 12:1 to "present our bodies a living sacrifice . . . unto God, which is our reasonable service" or "spiritual mode of worship" (Weymouth). Worship involves sacrifice.

Though the word *worship* is not used to describe Mary's act in John 12, the story of her offering gives us a beautiful example of worship. Jesus came to have dinner with Martha, Lazarus and Mary.

"Then took Mary a pound of ointment of spikenard, very costly, and anointed the feet of Jesus, and wiped his feet with her hair: and the house was filled with the odor of the ointment" (John 12:3).

Like Mary, when we kneel at His feet and pour out our worship in ministry to Him (notice that the ointment was costly), then He comes to us and the fragrance of His presence fills the sanctuaries of our lives.

WORSHIP INVOLVES FAITH, OBEDIENCE, PREPARATION, SEPARATION AND SACRIFICE UNTO HIM.

The Bible tells us more about HOW we are to worship God in John 4. Jesus met the Samaritan woman at Jacob's well.

She said, *"Sir, I perceive that thou art a prophet.*

"Our fathers worshipped in this mountain; and ye say, that in Jerusalem is the place where men ought to worship.

"Jesus saith unto her, Woman, believe me, the hour cometh, when ye shall neither in this mountain, nor yet at Jerusalem, worship the Father.

"Ye worship ye know not what: we know what we worship for salvation is of the Jews.

"But the hour cometh, and now is, when the true worshippers shall worship the Father in spirit and in truth: for the Father seeketh such to worship him.

"God is a Spirit: and they that worship him must worship him in spirit and in truth" (John 4:19-24).

In this passage we are given several insights regarding **where, who,** and **how** to worship.

Jesus emphasized that **true worship is inward, of the heart,** and not connected with any particular place, like Jerusalem or Mount Gerizim or any particular outward ritual.

He also emphasized that there are many people who worship idols and man-made conceptions of God but they do not know what they worship. However, Jesus said that the new breed of worshipers would be different, they would know the true God and worship Him in "spirit and in truth."

Jesus was the will of God in action. He said, "He that hath seen me, hath seen the Father" (John 14:9). **We know whom we worship only if we know the Jesus revealed in the Scriptures in a personal and intimate way.**

We express our worship to the Father in spirit, because the Holy Spirit has been given to us. And because Jesus is God and through Him we come to know our Heavenly Father, we are also enabled to worship God in truth.

We have said that worship is primarily inward, and that it is the disposition of the heart and not the location or posture of the body that is important.

Nevertheless, **God wants the body involved in worship.**

As we minister to Him, we find that our worship automatically finds expression through suitable attitudes of the body.

The most commonly used Hebrew word for "worship" is *shachah*, which means "to prostrate oneself" or "to bow down."

Eliezer, Abraham's servant, "bowed down his head and worshiped the Lord" (Genesis 24:26).

Moses "bowed his head toward the earth and worshiped" (Exodus 34:8) when God came down and stood with him on Mt. Sinai.

When Ezra blessed the Lord, "all the people answered Amen, Amen, with lifting up their hands: and they bowed their heads, and worshiped the Lord with their faces to the ground" (Nehemiah 8:6).

The psalmist exhorts us, "O come, let us worship and bow down: let us kneel before the Lord our Maker" (Psalm 95:6).

Though many times we stand and worship the Lord, as the people of Israel who "rose up and worshiped, every man in his tent door" (Exodus 33:10), we also often bow down and fall on our faces, prostrate before Him.

The most commonly used Greek work for worship is *proskuneo* which means, "I kiss toward" or "I kiss the hand toward." Often it is related to a falling down before God as the wise men who, when they saw Jesus, "fell down and worshiped him" (Matthew 2:11). Also as the women who, meeting the resurrected Jesus, fell down and "held Him by the feet and worshiped Him" (Matthew 28:9).

Paul, in worship and prayer, "bowed his knees" (Ephesians 3:14) unto God. He also exhorted us to "lift up holy hands without wrath and doubting" as we worship God (I Timothy 2:8).

When we worship and commune with God, there are times that we enter into a deep and living stillness where there are no words or sounds. There are times when He says to us, "Be still and know that I am God" (Psalm 46:10). Times when He commands us, "Stand in awe and sin not: commune with your own heart upon your bed and be still" (Psalm 4:4).

As He "maketh the storm a calm, so that the waves thereof are still" (Psalm 107:29), so He comes to us and we are stilled in His presence as we worship and commune with Him.

We do not have to minister to the Lord in any specific way. But there are a rich variety of ways to praise and worship Him, both individually and collectively, as we are led by the Holy Spirit.

First, we can praise and worship God with instruments.

Psalm 150 commands us to praise the Lord for His mighty acts and according to His excellent greatness. It lists all the known musical instruments in David's time and commands us to praise God on them.

"Praise Him with the sound of the trumpet (Hebrew—shophar: cornet, curved horn); *Praise Him with the psaltery* (Hebrew—nebel: a portable instrument of ten strings) *and harp* (Hebrew—kinnor: a portable harp or lyre of three to five strings).

"Praise Him with the timbrel (Hebrew—toph: tambourine, drum, tabret, tomtom), *and dance: praise Him with stringed instruments* (Hebrew—minnim: strings, like a zither) *and organs* (Hebrew—uggab: a wind instrument, like a flute).

"Praise Him upon the loud cymbals . . . upon the high sounding cymbals (Hebrew—tseltelim: hollow plates of brass).

"Let everything that hath breath praise the Lord. Praise ye the Lord" (Psalm 150).

When David and the 30,000 men of Israel went to bring the ark of God from Kirjath-jearim to Jerusalem, they put the ark of God on a new cart.

"David and all Israel played before God with all their might, and with singing . . . on all manner of instruments made of fir wood, even on harps, and on psalteries, and on timbrels, and on cornets and on cymbals" (II Samuel 6:1-5; I Chronicles 13:1-8).

Since David used every known instrument of his day to minister to the Lord, it seems obvious that we should be free to employ any of the instruments available to us today in our worship of God.

Secondly, and obviously, we use our vocal organs to praise and worship God in speaking, shouting, and singing His praises.

The psalmist said, "My mouth shall speak the praise of the Lord: and let all flesh bless His holy name for ever and ever" (Psalm 145:21).

"I will greatly praise the Lord with my mouth; yea, I will praise Him among the multitude" (Psalm 109:30).

"My soul shall be satisfied as with marrow and fatness; and my mouth shall praise thee with joyful lips" (Psalm 63:5).

"Let my mouth be filled with Thy praise and thy honor all the day" (Psalm 71:8).

"O Lord, open thou my lips; and my mouth shall shew forth thy praise" (Psalm 51:15).

When the temple foundation was laid, under Ezra, the priests put on their robes and blew their trumpets. "And the descendants of Asaph crashed their cymbals to praise the Lord in the manner ordained by King David. They sang rounds of praise and thanks to God, singing this song: 'He is good and His love and mercy toward Israel will last forever.' Then all the people gave a great shout, praising God because the foundation of the Temple had been laid" (Ezra 3:10-11 *The Living Bible*).

The psalmist writes, "O clap your hands, all ye people; shout unto God with the voice of triumph" (Psalm 47:1).

In a prayer to God, David asks, "Let thy priests be clothed with righteousness; and let thy saints shout for joy." God answers that He has chosen Zion and that He will "also clothe her priests with salvation; and her saints shall shout aloud for joy" (Psalm 132:9,16).

As God's priests we are not only to speak and shout His praises, but also to sing His praises.

The Apostle Paul tells us that we should "sing with grace in (our) hearts to the Lord" (Colossians 3:16).

If we are filled continually with the Holy Spirit, we will find ourselves "Speaking to (ourselves) in psalms, and hymns, and spiritual songs and singing and making melody in (our) hearts to the Lord" (Ephesians 5:19).

After Paul and Silas were beaten with many stripes (rods) and thrown into prison for casting a spirit of divination out of a girl, they prayed and sang hymns of praise (Greek—*humneo*) unto God. (Acts 16:25.)

The Psalms are full of admonitions to sing unto the Lord. For example, "O sing unto the Lord a new song; sing unto the Lord, all the earth. Sing unto the Lord, bless His name; shew forth His salvation from day to day" (Psalm 96:1-2).

Moses and the children of Israel sang unto the Lord after He delivered them from the Egyptians by bringing them through the Red Sea. (Exodux 15.)

Deborah and Barak sang praises unto God when He gave them victory over the Canaanites. (Judges 5.)

We too are to minister to God, to praise Him for His mighty works and His mercy towards us.

I believe that we should emphasize *ministering* choirs rather than *performing* choirs, in our churches today. We need choirs which sing and minister unto the Lord for just a long enough time to stir the congregation up to minister to the Lord also.

When David brought the ark of the covenant out of the house of Obed-edom and back to Jerusalem, he appointed singers and musicians to praise God before the ark.

"And David was clothed with a robe of fine linen, and all the Levites that bare the ark, and the singers, and Chenaniah the master of the song with the singers: David also had upon him an ephod of linen. Thus all Israel brought up the ark of the covenant of the Lord with shouting, and with sound of the cornet, and with trumpets, and with cymbals, making a noise with psalteries and harps" (I Chronicles 15:27-28).

How simple it is to see that in our time as well as David's time, it is as we first minister to God in praise and worship that His presence (like the ark) comes.

When the ark was at rest in Jerusalem, David set the chiefest of the fathers of Israel over the service of song in the house of the Lord. And they ministered before the Lord with their singing until Solomon had built the house of the Lord in Jerusalem and they waited on their office according to their order. (I Chronicles 6:31-33.)

David appointed these priests to sing unto the Lord (not to entertain the Israelites). They sang unto Him 24 hours a day. That is all that some of them, in fact the chiefest of them, were employed to do. Sometimes they used instruments and added these to their praise and worship. These priests ministered unto the Lord "according to their order" day and night until Solomon built the temple in Jerusalem.

When Solomon dedicated the temple he added 120 priests sounding trumpets to the 288 Levites who were the singers or musicians appointed by David.

As we have mentioned, it was when the priests "were as one, to make one sound to be heard in praising and thanking the Lord . . . that then the house was filled with a cloud, even the house of the Lord; so that the priests could not stand to minister by reason of the cloud: for the glory of the Lord had filled the house of God" (II Chronicles 5:11-14).

The glory came down, not when they built the temple, or offered the sacrifices, but when they ministered to the Lord.

Both David and Solomon realized the priority of ministering to the Lord. Solomon continued his father's religious policies. During his reign the priests continued to minister before the Lord night and day with praise and thanksgiving and worship.

Should we not as priests unto God under this new and better covenant do at least as well in ministering to the Lord as the priests of God under the old covenant?

In ministering to the Lord, we are often exhorted to use our hands.

The psalmist writes, "O clap your hands all ye people; shout unto God with the voice of triumph" (Psalm 47:1).

Even the floods are told to be joyful in view of the Lord's coming to judge the earth, and to "clap their hands" (Psalm 98:8).

Isaiah writes that when Israel would be regathered into the land from all nations the mountains would break forth into singing and all the trees of the field would clap their hands. (Isaiah 55:12.)

We can express our joy to God as we minister to Him by **clapping our hands**.

Also, we are exhorted to **lift up our hands** as we praise Him.

The Bible says, *"Behold, bless ye the Lord all ye servants of the Lord, which by night stand in the house of the Lord. Lift up your hands in the sanctuary, and bless the Lord"* (Psalm 134:1-2).

We are not supposed to sit on our hands. We are to use them for the glory of God. Lazarus was bound hand to foot, but we are free, free to use our hands for the glory of God.

Paul said in his letter to Timothy, "I will therefore that men pray everywhere, lifting up holy hands without wrath and doubting" (I Timothy 2:8).

Holy hands, clean hands, speak of a clean heart and life. Thus, we must be washed in the blood of Jesus and with the Word of God before we come into God's presence.

The psalmist prayed, "Let my prayer be set before thee as incense; and the lifting up of my hands as the evening sacrifice" (Psalm 141:2).

After Solomon had dedicated the temple to the Lord, he "stood before the altar of the Lord in the presence of all the congregation of Israel, and spread forth his hands toward heaven and prayed" (II Chronicles 6:12).

Ezra in a prayer of intercession, "fell on his knees and spread out his hands unto the Lord his God" (Ezra 9:5).

Use those hands, bless the Lord and lift them up in His name. (Psalm 63:4.) Lift them up unto Him. Lift them up unto His commandments. Get them away from trying to manipulate. Lift them up to God, and His river of power and life will flow.

We can praise God in so many ways. We can praise God *lying down*. The Bible says, "Let the saints be joyful in glory: let them sing aloud upon their beds" (Psalm 149:5).

We are exhorted to praise God's name in the *dance* and praise Him with musical instruments and dance (Psalm 149:3; 150:4).

We praise God *standing up* and *bowing down*. "Praise ye the Lord . . . O ye servants of the Lord . . . that stand in the house of our Lord" (Psalm 135:1-2).

God says of the "priests the Levites, the sons of Zadok . . . they shall come near to me to minister unto me, and they shall stand before me to offer unto me the fat and the blood . . ." (Ezekiel 44:15).

When Solomon prayed the dedicatory prayer of the temple, he *"kneeled* down upon his knees before all the congregation of Israel, and spread forth his hands toward heaven . . ." (II Chronicles 6:13).

David writes, "O come, let us worship and bow down: let us *kneel* before the Lord our maker" (Psalm 95:6).

Daniel *kneeled* toward Jerusalem "upon his knees three times a day, and prayed, and gave thanks before his God . . ." (Daniel 6:10).

Even Jesus *kneeled* down when He prayed. (Luke 22:41.)

As we have mentioned, in praise as in worship, we sometimes bow our heads or prostrate ourselves before the Lord. Certainly there are times that no matter what the attitude of our bodies, our souls are on their knees. But God does want us to use our bodies to express our worship to Him wherever possible.

We do not have to minister to the Lord in any specific way. But there are certainly a rich variety of ways to express our praise and worship to Him as we are led by the Spirit.

4
Some Results Of Ministering To The Lord

There are many results of ministering to the Lord, but we will only discuss some of these briefly.

Sometimes worship culminates in revelation, though normally revelation leads to worship.

When Moses went up to Mount Sinai, "The Lord descended in the cloud, and stood with him there, and proclaimed the name of the Lord. . .(then) Moses made haste and bowed his head toward the earth, and worshipped" (Exodus 34:5,8). When Moses saw God, his response was one of worship.

When Jesus healed the man who was blind from birth, the man was questioned by the Pharisees, thrown out of the synagogue, and later found by Jesus. When Jesus told the man that HE was the Son of God, the blind man responded with worship. He said, "Lord, I believe. And he worshipped Him" (John 9:38).

There are innumerable examples of those who saw God and then worshiped Him. Abraham, Jeremiah, Isaiah, Daniel, all saw the Lord in one way or another and worshiped.

When we see God, whether it be in His Word, through a manifestation of His power, or through some visitation experience, our automatic response is one of worship.

Not only does the revelation of God to us evoke a response of worship, but often it is as we worship and commune with God that He chooses to reveal Himself and unfold His truths to us. In other words, **worship often leads to revelation.**

Take, for example, the case of Anna, in Luke 2. As Anna worshiped the Lord and waited upon Him, God showed her many of His secrets. He showed her much about Jesus; for as she saw the baby Jesus in the temple, she "spake of Him to all them that looked for redemption in Jerusalem" (Luke 2:38).

As the leaders of the church in Antioch gathered together and ministered to the Lord, the Holy Spirit spoke and revealed God's will to them in the matter of Barnabas and Saul. He said, "Separate me Barnabas and Saul for the work whereunto I have called them" (Acts 13:1-2). Their worship led to a revelation from God.

Isaiah was probably praying in the temple when he had his tremendous experience of seeing God.

"In the year that king Uzziah died I saw also the Lord sitting upon a throne, high and lifted up, and his train filled the temple.

"*Above it stood the seraphims: each one had six wings; with twain he covered his face, and with twain he covered his feet, and with twain he did fly.*

"*And one cried unto another and said, Holy, holy, holy, is the Lord of hosts: the whole earth is full of his glory.*

"*And the posts of the door moved at the voice of him that cried, and the house was filled with smoke.*

"*Then said I, Woe is me! for I am undone; because I am a man of unclean lips, and I dwell in the midst of a people of unclean lips: for mine eyes have seen the King, the Lord of hosts.*

"*Then flew one of the seraphims unto me, having a live coal in his hand, which he had taken with the tongs from off the altar:*

"*And he laid it upon my mouth, and said, Lo, this hath touched thy lips; and thine iniquity is taken away, and thy sin purged.*

"*Also I heard the voice of the Lord, saying, Whom shall I send, and who will go for us? Then said I, Here am I; send me*" (Isaiah 6:1-8).

Isaiah had a revelation of the holiness of God. God was holy, high and lifted up. He was awesome in His grandeur, splendor, and majesty. Even the seraphim covered their faces and feet and cried, "Holy."

It is interesting to note that the seraphim used four wings to cover themselves and two wings to fly.

In other words, one could say that they put twice as much emphasis on worship as on work. We have already seen that our work flows from our worship.

Also, they said, "Holy" three times to signify the holiness of each member of the Trinity.

They also did this when John saw them. "And the four beasts had each one of them six wings about him; and they were full of eyes within: and they rest not day and night, saying, "Holy, holy, holy, Lord God Almighty, which was, and is, and is to come" (Revelation 4:8).

When the word of the Lord came to Jeremiah and God commissioned him to be a prophet to the nations, Jeremiah felt deeply inadequate. He said, "Ah, Lord God! behold, I cannot speak: for I am a child" (Jeremiah 1:6).

Moses felt the same stinging reality of his own inadequacy when God appeared to him at the burning bush and called him to deliver the Hebrews out of Egypt.

He said, "*Who am I that I should go unto Pharaoh, and that I should bring forth the children of Israel out of Egypt? O my Lord, I am not eloquent, neither heretofore, nor since thou hast spoken unto thy servant: but I am slow of speech, and of a slow tongue*" (Exodus 3:11; 4:10).

Job too was humbled after he saw God. He said to Him, "I have uttered (things) that I understood not; things too wonderful for me, which I knew not. I have heard of thee by the hearing of the ear: but now mine eye seeth thee. Wherefore I abhor myself and repent in dust and ashes" (Job 42:3, 5-6). Job worshiped and saw God.

Like Isaiah, Jeremiah, Moses, Job and others, we need a revelation of the living God. We need to be caught up in the wonder of His Person as we worship Him. We need to be ignited with His power and glimpse His holiness and splendor if He is to use us. This often begins with worship.

Not only does worship bring us into revelation of God, His purposes and plans, and of who we are, but **worship brings us into one accord, into the unity of the Spirit.**

As we worship the Lord with many other Christians, we are brought into a unity, a oneness. Instead of concentrating on our differences, we look at Jesus and focus on Him. As we are caught up in the wonder of His Person, those differences pale beside Him. It is as we look together to Jesus and worship Him that we are drawn closer to Him and to each other.

Someone has said that it is as if Christians are arranged in a circle around God like spokes near the outer rim of a wheel. As we each draw closer to God, approaching the hub of the wheel, so also we draw closer to each other.

Worshiping God brings us into one accord.

Paul exhorted the Colossians to "hold the Head," to look to Jesus and lift Him up and not concentrate on petty human ordinances and do's and don'ts. Paul said that if we lift up Jesus and keep our focus on Him, we will all receive God's nourishment, be knit together and increase with the increase of God. (Colossians 2:19.)

Throughout the books of Acts, we see that the early Christians were in one accord, and as they waited upon the Lord together and worshiped Him, they were kept in one accord.

Worshiping the Lord not only brings a unity among Christians, but it releases the flow of God's life and power.

There is a power in praise and worship that pushes back the satanic and releases the Divine, and that brings our minds into captivity to Jesus Christ. God "inhabits the praises of His people." As we praise Him, the power of the Spirit is stirred up within us and moves out from us pushing the enemy back.

I used to spend a great deal of time rebuking the devil. Now I just rebuke him one time and begin to praise and worship God. Then the devil is automatically pushed back as the Holy Spirit is released within me and flows out from me.

We see a good example of this in II Chronicles 20 when Moab, Ammon and Edom came against Judah and her king, Jehoshaphat. Jehoshaphat stood in the congregation of Judah and asked God what to do in view of the impending battle.

God answered and said, "Be not afraid nor dismayed by reason of this great multitude; for the battle is not yours, but God's. Ye shall not need to fight in this battle; set yourselves, stand ye still, and see the salvation of the Lord with you, O Judah and Jerusalem" (II Chronicles 20:15, 17).

On the day of battle, Jehoshaphat "appointed singers unto the Lord, and that should praise the beauty of holiness, as they went out before the army, and to say, Praise the Lord: for His mercy endureth forever. And when they began to sing and to praise, the Lord set ambushments against the children of Ammon, Moab and Mount Seir, which were come against Judah; and they were smitten" (II Chronicles 20:21-22). In fact, the Ammonites, Moabites and the inhabitants of Mount Seir killed one another!

I believe that as God's people came against the enemy, their spirits were lifted up in praise and worship. They were moved from the natural into the supernatural realm, singing the Lord's songs, the songs that the Holy Spirit created through them even as they were being sung. As they ministered to the Lord, the Lord moved through them and pushed back their enemies.

Praise and worship release the power and life of God.

When Paul and Silas were beaten and imprisoned for preaching the gospel and freeing a demon-possessed girl, they sang praises to God. The result was that God's power was released.

"Suddenly there was a great earthquake, so that the foundations of the prison were shaken: and immediately all the doors were opened, and every one's bands were loosed" (Acts 16:26). Their praise released a power that opened the prison doors.

As we praise God today, power is unleashed that heals, delivers, and bursts open the doors that the enemy has tried to shut.

When the early disciples praised and prayed to the Lord, "the place was shaken where they were assembled together; and they were all filled with the Holy Ghost, and they spake the word of God with boldness" (Acts 4:24-31). God's life and power are released as we praise and worship Him.

We are vehicles through which the life and power of God can flow into this dark world. Jesus is the life, and as we come to Him and drink, that life flows into us. Then, as we praise and worship God, that life flows out of us toward God. As we obey God and move by faith, that life flows through us into the deserts of the world.

Jesus stood up and cried during the last day of the Feast of Tabernacles, "If any man thirst, let him come unto Me and drink. He that believeth on Me, as the Scripture hath said, out of his belly shall flow rivers of living water" (John 7:37-38). Jesus was referring to the fullness of the Holy Spirit that would be given to Christians after He was glorified (verse 39).

When we come to Jesus and drink, an inflow of life is established. God also wants to establish an outflow of life. God does not want us merely to receive life; but to come to the place where He can impart the life of the Holy Spirit through us, the place where His life flows out from us to others.

Adam received the life of God and was made a living soul. Jesus, the "last Adam, was made a quickening (or life-giving) spirit" (I Corinthians 15:45).

God doesn't just want you to receive life, or to make you live, He wants to put the same Spirit in you that was in Jesus, so that out of the Holy Spirit in you will flow rivers of life-giving water. **God is interested both in an inflow and an outflow of life.**

Jesus picked a very important time, at the Feast of Tabernacles, to say that if we would come to Him and drink, rivers of living water would flow forth out of our innermost beings.

He chose to say this during the time when the priests poured water from the pool of Siloam, mingled with wine, upon the morning sacrifice which laid upon the altar.

If the priests would have poured enough water upon the altar, that water would have run down through the altar and into the outer court, through the gates of the temple, the streets of the city, out into the Kidron Valley and down into the Dead Sea.

It was while the priests were pouring water mixed with wine on the altar and the people were singing with great joy that Jesus stood up and cried, "If any man thirst, let him come unto Me and drink. He that believeth on Me, as the Scripture hath said, out of his belly shall flow rivers of living water" (John 7:37-38).

Jesus releases His rivers of living water through us as we come to Him and drink. As we worship and obey Him, these rivers flow Godward and manward, respectively.

Ezekiel saw a vision of the increasing, swelling River of God coming out of the Millennial Temple in Jerusalem. And "behold, waters issued out from under the threshold of the house eastward" (Ezekiel 47:1), and flowed to the right side of the altar and along on the south side of the eastern passageway and eventually into the east country and the desert. It divided some point south of Jerusalem into two rivers, one river flowing into the Mediterranean Sea and the other into the Dead Sea.

There is no outflow of water from the Dead Sea. It is dead *because there is no outlet.* This is true of many people's lives also and that is why they are spiritually dead.

But God's River is going to run into the Dead Sea and the waters are going to be healed. There will be an outlet and inflow of the Mediterranean Sea into the Dead Sea and a very great multitude of fish will come into the Dead Sea.

Since an ocean or sea in the Bible signifies a mass of humanity, the Dead Sea signifies a mass of spiritually dead humanity. But God is going to cause His increasing swelling River of Life to flow into the great mass of unregenerate humanity. They will drink of that river of life and be healed.

God is bringing forth "rivers in the desert (and) waters in the wilderness to give drink to (His) people" (Isaiah 43:19-20). As the hungry and thirsty come unto Him and drink, His life will flow into them and they will worship God in a river of praise. Then they will move out to obey Him, doing exploits in the power of the Spirit.

Ezekiel saw the increasing, swelling River of God beginning as a little stream and growing into a huge river about three miles wide. This is what is happening to some degree in our time.

Worshiping the Lord not only releases the flow of His life and power through us, but it keeps us in balance, spiritually. It also helps us to keep everything in a proper perspective in our lives.

We need to focus more on the *person* of God than on His *blessings*, and more on *His life* than on *the forms* through which that life flows.

It is time to let God arise. It is time to put Him first and not ourselves and our ideas and emphasis.

How often we ridicule the pagan world which worships and serves the creature more than the Creator. (Romans 1:25.)

How often we point our fingers at the Pharisees, who worshiped the forms God gave them (which pointed to the Reality to come), so that when indeed Christ came, they rejected Him for the forms.

Do we not do the same thing?

So many people today have different idols, idols that they exalt above the person of God himself. These may be spiritual methods, gifts, orders, revelations, hobbyhorses. But whatever they be, if we look to them for renewal instead of to Him, they are idols.

Many times in history, God has used people, programs and things as vehicles for His power. But very often, men end up by worshiping and clinging to the form while the life of God moves on. Men often turn from the life to the form that has contained the life. They did it in the Old Testament and many of us do it today.

Someone has pointed out that in Numbers 21, when the people of Israel were bitten by fiery serpents in the desert, Moses was told to make a serpent of brass. He "put it on a pole, and it came to pass, that if a serpent had bitten any man, when he behold the serpent of brass, he lived" (Numbers 21:9).

The life of God moved through that serpent of brass. When the people beheld it, they were healed. But Israel forgot the life and clung to the form.

For 900 years, Israel worshiped that brazen serpent and burned incense to it until Hezekiah broke it in pieces.

For Hezekiah "removed the high places, and brake the images, and cut down the groves, and brake in pieces the brasen serpent that Moses had made: for unto those days the children of Israel did burn incense to it: and he called it Nehushtan (a thing of brass)" (II Kings 18:4).

The children of Israel were worshiping the vehicle or instrument God used more than the Source, God Himself.

Don't we do this today?

When we put programs, revelations, methods, anything above God himself, then we become unbalanced, we cling to lifeless forms, and the life of God moves on without us.

But if we minister to Him first and put Him first, then our lives will be continually enriched by Him and made channels of blessing to others

You can never love Him too much. You can never spend too much time with Him, for your first ministry is to Him. He is worthy to receive "glory and honor and power: for (He) has created all things, and for (His) pleasure they are and were created" (Revelation 4:11).

If you are interested in having a crusade or a teaching conference in your church or area, or you desire a list of Rev. Brant's cassette tapes, contact:

Coordinator of Ministries
Roxanne Brant Ministries
P.O. Box 1000
O'Brien, Florida 32071
(904) 935-0948

CLIP OUT ORDER FORM

NUMBER	TITLE	PRICE
_____	How to Test Prophecy, Preaching and Guidance	$5.50
_____	The Growing Power of Faith	$3.95
_____	Ministering to the Lord	$3.95
_____	Guidance [6-Cassette Series with Folder]	$25.00
_____	Recent Angelic Visitations	$1.50
_____	8 Biblical Ways to Receive Healing	$5.50
_____	Transported by the Holy Spirit (Book)	$1.50
_____	The Jim Kaseman Story *NEW*	$1.50
_____	Rivers of Evidence	$2.95
$_____	ADD $1.00 (POSTAGE)	
$_____	SUBTOTAL	
$_____	TOTAL ENCLOSED	
	MINIMUM ORDER — $4.00	

Order from and make checks payable to:

Roxanne Brant Ministries
P.O. Box 1000
O'Brien, Florida 32071

Send Materials to (PLEASE PRINT):

NAME _____

ADDRESS _____

CITY _____

STATE _____ ZIP CODE_____

(Standard trade discounts available to bookstores.)

212 pages

105 pages

195 pages

Read the above and learn **THE GROWING POWER OF FAITH,** the levels of faith, the multiplying potential of faith and how to increase your faith in every area of life. Learn **HOW TO TEST PROPHECY, PREACHING AND GUIDANCE** to discover the process and results of testing spiritual phenomena and be able to distinguish the genuine from the counterfeit by applying Scriptural tests to all ministry. Learn how you can receive healing through **8 BIBLICAL WAYS TO RECEIVE HEALING.** These will change your life!

(Order using CLIP OUT ORDER FORM on page 95.)